Minibeast Pets
Ants

by Theresa Greenaway

Photographs by Chris Fairclough

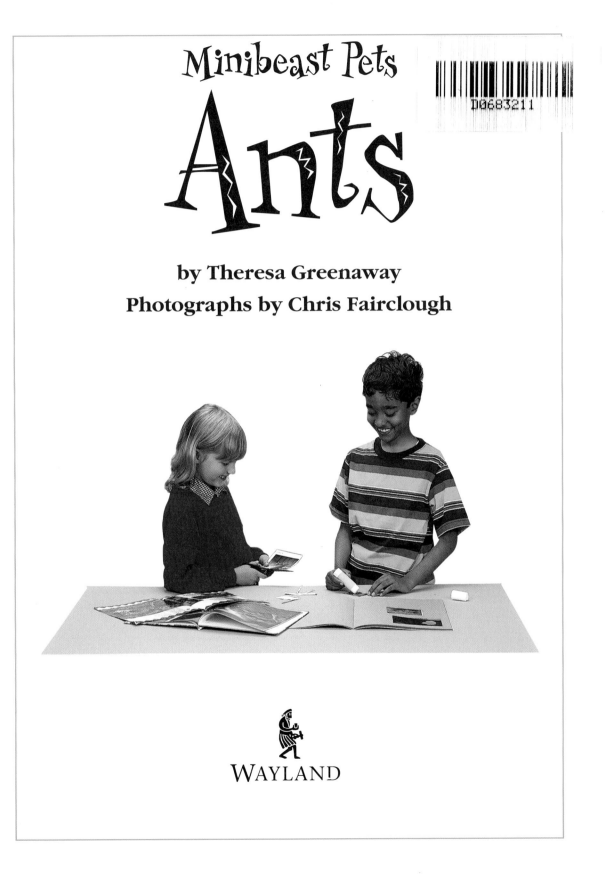

WAYLAND

Minibeast Pets

Beetles
Caterpillars
Centipedes and Millipedes
Slugs and Snails

Spiders
Tadpoles
Worms

Cover photograph: Leaf cutter ants carrying a section of leaf.

All Wayland books encourage
children to read and help them improve their literacy.

- ✓ The contents page, page numbers, headings, diagrams and index help locate specific pieces of information.

- ✓ The glossary reinforces alphabetic knowledge and extends vocabulary.

- ✓ On page 30 you can find out about other books, videos, CD-ROMs and websites dealing with the same subject.

© Copyright 2000 (text) Wayland Publishers Limited
61 Western Road, Hove, East Sussex BN3 1JD

Planned and produced by Discovery Books Limited
Project Editors: Patience Coster and Pam Wells
Project Manager: Joyce Spicer
Illustrated by Colin Newman and Stefan Chabluk
Designed by Ian Winton

British Library Cataloguing in Publication Data
Greenaway, Theresa, 1947-
    Ants. – (Minibeast Pets)
    1. Ants – Juvenile literature
    2. Ants as pets – Juvenile literature
    I. Title
    595.7'96

HARDBACK   ISBN 0 7502 2688 9
PAPERBACK   ISBN 0 7502 2742 7

Printed and bound in the USA

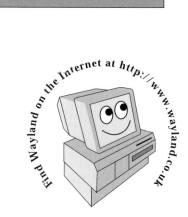

Find Wayland on the Internet at http://www.wayland.co.uk

WARNING
Some ants bite. Do not pick them up with your bare hands unless you know they do not bite. Ask an adult to help you identify which types of ants can bite.

Contents

Ants everywhere

There are about 9,500 different kinds of ants. They live all around the world except in water or where it is too cold. But some ants are found inside the Arctic Circle.

Ants seem to go everywhere, and there are so many of them! They live in gardens, forests, farms, under walkways, and sometimes in houses and kitchens. Some live high in the treetops, others live deep underground.

Small – but fierce!

Most types of ants will attack much larger animals, including humans, by biting with their jaws. Then, the ant twists its abdomen and squirts a stinging liquid into the bite. Just one bite and squirt may not be much, but when hundreds attack, it hurts!

Each ant has a long body divided into segments, six legs, and a head armed with biting or snipping mouthparts. Only the males and young queen ants have wings.

abdomen
The ant stings or squirts stinging liquid from the tip of its abdomen.

thorax
The part of the ant to which the legs are attached.

jaws
An ant attacks by biting.

antennae
An ant can smell as well as feel with its antennae.

mouth
An ant cuts up its food before swallowing it.

An ant's life

Ants are insects. They make their nests in many different places. Some may live under large stones or pieces of slate.

Others build a nest among the roots of plants. They pile up small pieces of soil around the plant stems. In woodlands, different kinds of ants make huge mounds of earth over their nests.

▲ Some kinds of ants build their nests high up in the branches of a tree.

How ants develop

1. The queen ant lays eggs.

2. The eggs hatch into grubs (larvae). The worker ants look after the eggs and grubs.

Within the ants' nest there may be one or more queen ants, new queens, male ants and thousands of worker ants. Some kinds of ants also produce large soldier ants.

When a queen has mated, she stores the sex cells from a male in her body. She allows some of these to fertilize eggs that will become females, workers, or new queens. Unfertilized eggs become males.

Ants' eggs hatch into tiny, helpless grubs. These grow and moult until they are ready to pupate, or change. Inside the pupa, the grub changes into an adult ant.

The worker ants look after the queen, her eggs and grubs.

3. The grubs spin cocoons around themselves. Inside these cocoons, they change into pupae.

4. Young ants hatch from the cocoons. The ants' bodies gradually harden and darken.

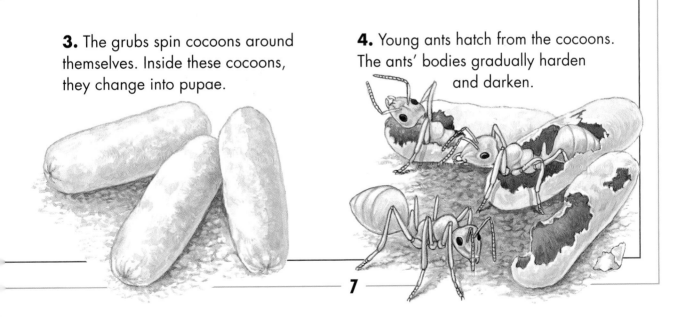

Life in an ant colony

Ants are called 'social' insects. This is because they live in large groups called colonies. In colonies, ants work together as a team. Most of the ants in a colony are workers. These are females who cannot lay eggs. Since they have all come from the same queen ant, they are sisters. Worker ants look after the queen, bringing her food, and keeping her safe. They look after the eggs and grubs, too.

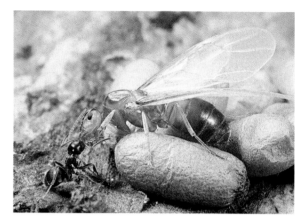

▲ This young, winged queen has just hatched from a pupa.

Keeping the eggs clean

Moving pupae

Laying eggs

◄ An ant's nest is made up of many chambers. Some chambers are close to the surface of the ground, others may be deep underground.

Super ants!

Young wood ant queens return to their home nest and make a new colony that is connected to it. In Hokkaido, Japan, a 'super colony' of wood ants spread over 2.7 square kilometres (just under half the size of a football pitch!).

Worker ants collect food from outside the nest and take it home to feed the grubs. They make sure that the grubs are kept at the right temperature. The worker ants carry grubs up to the surface when it is warm, and take them deep below ground when there is a frost. Worker ants do not live very long, but the queens may live for over twenty years.

Some colonies have more than one queen. If there is only one, when she dies, the whole colony will slowly die. But by that time, the old queen will have produced hundreds of new queens, who may have started their own colonies.

Homes for ants

Before you collect any ants, ask an adult to help you make a home for them. You will need a deep, clear plastic container. An aquarium would be perfect.

Ask an adult to drill small holes in the bottom. Stand the container in a watertight tray. Put finely crumbled earth into the container, leaving a 5 cm gap at the top.

Team work

Many types of ants catch living prey, but they also eat the bodies of insects that have already died. If a dead fly or beetle is too large for one ant to carry, then a group of ants works as a team to take the corpse back to the nest.

Carefully pour a little water into the tray, so that the container is standing in a moat. If you are using an aquarium with a ridge around the bottom, make sure that the water is just deep enough to cover the holes in the base. The water will stop the ants if they manage to escape from the container.

Your container will need a removable but tight-fitting lid, with airholes small enough to prevent ants from escaping. If the holes in the lid are too large, line it with a piece of plain cotton cloth. Remember that ants are very good at escaping. You will need a lid that is quick and easy to take off and put back on, otherwise there will be ants everywhere!

Finding ants

Look for an ants' nest under large stones or among plant roots. Make notes about the ants you see. Decide which type of ants you want to keep. Some types are much fiercer than others and will bite. If you do not know which ones bite, ask an adult.

When you are ready to start collecting ants, ask a friend or an adult to go with you. Make sure you have something to put the ants into, such as jars or other containers with small airholes in their lids. Collect a spade, a trowel, and a little plastic pot that can be used as a scoop.

Ant language

Ants 'talk' to each other using signs, touches, but most of all, smells. Glands in an ant's head, and others at the tip of its abdomen release a whole range of different smells. These smells may say, "I have found food", "Be careful, enemy suspected", or "Attack!". Ants pick up these smells with their sensitive antennae.

Take the collecting equipment to the site of the ants' nest you have chosen. The easiest kinds of ants to catch and keep are those living in parks or gardens. They make their nests in the earth.

◀ Ants often make their nests under rocks, because the rock may help the soil to stay warm.

Collecting ants

Ants can only survive as a colony. Ants without a queen do not really know what to do. They just scurry around, running in every direction, until they die. So to keep ants as pets, you must catch a queen along with some of the workers.

There are two ways to find a queen ant. In mid-to late summer, you can collect a young queen as she lands after her marriage flight. This is when she prepares to snap off her wings. Or you can carefully dig into an ants' nest until the queen is uncovered.

▲ Use a spade to dig deep into the ants' nest.

Have everything ready. Carefully dig up as much of the nest as you can. Hundreds of angry workers will swarm everywhere.

When you spot the large, wingless queen, with her stomach swollen with eggs, gently scoop her up and put her into a container. You will have to catch her quickly, before she burrows underground. Put the lid on the container so that she cannot escape. Then collect as many of her workers, eggs, and grubs as possible. Put them into the same container, or another one if this is easier. Take your ants home immediately.

▲ Ants run around so quickly that it is difficult to scoop them up.

Ants on the march

Colonies of army ants are found in the tropics of North, Central, and South America. They only stay in the same place for a short time. Three weeks is just long enough for the queen to lay thousands of eggs. When these hatch, the workers pick up the grubs and the whole colony moves to a new place. When they are on the move, the workers kill all insects and small animals in their path.

Starting your colony

Take the lid off your new ant home and gently but quickly pour all the ants, including the queen, on to the soil. Cover it again immediately. Watch what happens through the sides of the plastic box.

▶ Tip the ants on to the soil. Once they have recovered, the ants will carefully rebuild their colony.

The ants will run around frantically for a while, but then they will start to look after their queen.

The ants will take the eggs and grubs down into the soil.
Then they will start to rebuild their colony. As they tunnel into the soil to make new chambers, you will be able to watch what happens through the sides of the box.

Wrap the sides of your ant home with black paper to keep it dark. Keep the paper away from the moat or it will get soggy. Do not put paper over the lid. Encouraged by the darkness, the ants may build tunnels at the sides of the container. When you want to watch your tiny pets, just remove the paper.

At first, you may not see much, because the colony will be so small. As it grows, the queen will start to fill the new home with eggs. She will stay buried in the soil of her home, while the workers go up to the surface to hunt for food. Look for little holes in the soil. These are the entrances to tunnels leading down into the nest.

▲ A worker ant clears pieces of soil away from a nest entrance.

Feeding ants

Most common types of garden ants are easy to feed. They will eat dead insects, and cat or dog food. Most love sweet things like sugar or honey. Put little piles of different kinds of food on top of the soil in your ant home. Remember to put the lid back on, or the ants will escape.

Workers will soon find the food. They will be able to smell it with their antennae. You will soon find out what they like best. Take out anything that the ants really do not like or it will go mouldy.

Sink a small lid filled with water into the soil. This will give the ants something to drink. The ants' nest container is standing in water for two reasons. Some of the water will soak up through the holes drilled in the bottom of the container. This will keep the soil just damp enough for the ants. It will also stop any ants that crawl under the lid from escaping.

Ant gardeners

Tropical leaf-cutter ants grow their own food. Large workers snip pieces of leaves and carry them to underground chambers in their nest. Small workers put the leaf pieces into a 'garden', where a white, fluffy fungus grows on the leaves. The ants eat the fungus.

Watching ants

Ants make fascinating pets. If your colony is successful, you will be able to watch their daily lives through the clear plastic sides of their home. Keep a scrapbook or an ant-watching diary. Record how the colony settles in and grows.

At the same time, watch what the other ants are doing in your garden or neighbourhood. Some kinds of ants 'milk' sap-sucking aphids that live on garden plants.

▼ Ants stroke aphids and drink the sugary liquid the aphids produce.

The ant strokes the aphid, which produces a little droplet of sugary liquid at the tip of its abdomen. This is called honeydew, and the ants drink it.

Watch what happens when two different kinds of ants meet. Do they run away from each other, or do they fight? How do they fight? You will need a magnifying glass to see exactly what happens. If you want to find out more about ants, look for books and CD-ROMs in your library, and on the Internet. See the list on page 30.

Stinging ants
Australian bulldog ants are just one of many kinds of ants that have a sting. They are large. The worker ants are 3 cm long. Each has powerful jaws that grip a victim's skin. Then, the ant injects a painful venom with its stinger.

Flying ants

Deep in the ants' nest, the queen lays some eggs that grow into queen and male ants with wings. Workers look after these winged ants until one warm, damp day in summer, when they crawl outside the nest and fly off.

◄ These winged ants will take off and fly high into the air.

As winged ants from all the nests in the area take off, the air becomes full of flying ants. Ants fly so that males from one nest can meet and mate with unrelated females from another nest. The male ant's life is very short. Soon after he has mated, he dies.

The young, mated queen flies back to earth and snaps off her wings. She is ready to start a new colony, but first she has to find the right place.

If your ant colony is successful, it too will produce ants with wings. When this happens, take the colony outside, and let them fly away.

Ants in winter

Ants do not like the cold. There are many more ants in hot, dry deserts than there are in cold places, such as on the tops of mountains. In parts of the world that have cold winters, life can get difficult for a large ant colony. In very low temperatures, the surface layer of the ground may freeze solid. There is not much food for the ants to find.

Water carriers

Giant hunting ants of Central and South America prevent their grubs from dying of thirst in the dry season. Worker ants collect drops of water from dew and carry them back to the nest between their jaws. The grubs and ants in the nest can drink this water.

Many kinds of ants that live in places with cold winters make nests that reach deep into the ground. As winter approaches, these ants move their queen and the grubs deeper and deeper, so the frost cannot reach them. Plant material taken into the nest heats up as it rots. This helps to keep the centre of the nest warm. The whole colony is much less active in winter.

See what happens in your colony, but do not keep it outside, or all the ants will die. Try to find out what happens to ants that live in warm countries. Tropical parts of the world do not have winters, but they often have a dry season. Sometimes this lasts for months.

▲ Ants stay deep underground until the spring sunshine warms the soil.

Letting them go

When you have found out all you can from your ant colony, it is time to let them out into the wild again. Perhaps you might like to keep a different kind of ant, or another kind of minibeast pet altogether.

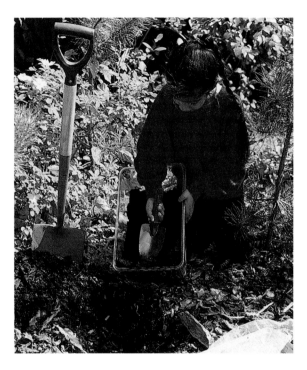

Check in your notebook to see where you collected your ants. A new colony may have moved into the place occupied by your ants. Do not let your ants out here, or they will fight the other ants. Try to find a sheltered spot nearby where there do not seem to be any ants. Dig a hole, and gently slide your ants into it. Cover them with leaves. They will soon organize a new nest.

Ants are tiny, but they can lift things that weigh much more than themselves, such as a heavy grub or pupa. Whenever a nest is disturbed, workers snatch up grubs, eggs, and pupae and carry them away to a safe place.

▼ If grubs or pupae are uncovered, the workers pick them up in their jaws and carry them to safety.

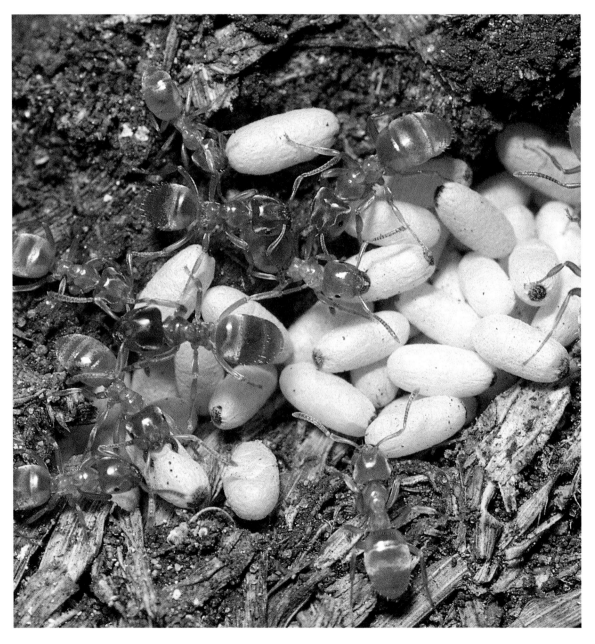

Ant facts

Some of the workers of honey ants are called 'repletes'. 'Replete' means 'full'. These ants store the nectar and honeydew that other workers bring back to the nest. The abdomens of the repletes swell until they are huge. These ants hang from the sides of the nest. They are used as storage containers to feed the rest of the colony in times when food is scarce. Repletes are sometimes kidnapped by ants from other nests.

▲ Each 'replete' ant is swollen with stored honeydew.

Anteaters depend on ants for food. This anteater is digging for ants under a tree stump. It has a very long tongue, which it uses to lick up its prey.

◄ Anteaters do not seem to mind being bitten by ants.

Trapdoor ants have very long, saw-like jaws. These open wide and snap shut very fast on moving prey, such as tiny springtails. One type of trapdoor ant can shut its jaws in less than one-thousandth of a second!

Aztec ants live in the hollow stems of Cecropia trees, which grow in tropical South America. The trees provide them with nectar from special glands. In return, the aztec ants fiercely prevent any other insects from eating the trees' leaves or harming them.

Weaver ants of Africa and Southeast Asia live in forests. Just one colony may occupy the leaves, branches, and trunks of seventeen large trees!

▲ Fierce aztec ants attack anything that touches their tree – even people!

In the south-west USA, large numbers of harvester ants fly to patches of ground to mate. There are more males than females. Balls of ants build up as males cluster around a female, trying to mate.

Finding out more

BOOKS

Bug Books: Ants (Heinemann, 1998)

Eyewitness 3D: Insect (Dorling Kindersley, 1998)

My Best Book of Creepy Crawlies by Claire Llewellyn (Kingfisher, 1998)

Spotters Guides: Insects (Usborne, 1999)

CD-ROMS

Insects: Little Creatures in a Big World (Ransom Publishing, 1997)

WEBSITES

The Bug Club
http://www.ex.ac.uk/bugclub/

The Yuckiest Site on the Internet
http://www.yucky.com

VIDEOS

Amazing Animals: Creepy Crawly Animals /Minibeasts (Dorling Kindersley, 1999/1996)

See How They Grow: Minibeasts (Dorling Kindersley, 1999)

FURTHER INFORMATION

Ask your teacher to contact CLEAPPS School Science Service for information on any aspect of keeping minibeasts. Tel: 01895 251496.

Contact the national Wildlife Trust office to find out about joining your local Wildlife Watch Group. Tel: 01636 677711.

SCIENCE
Observing minibeasts
Animal classification / variation
Animal habitats
Life cycles
Life processes
Moving and growing
Food chains / nutrition
Animal adaptations
Animal behaviour
Use of magnifying glass

ENGLISH
Following instructions
Recording observations
Using glossaries
Extending scientific vocabulary
Research skills

ART, DESIGN & TECHNOLOGY
Close observation: drawings of minibeasts
Investigating camouflage / mimicry
Designing and making (scrapbooks, containers for minibeasts)

Minibeast Pets
TOPIC WEB

MATHS
Measuring skills
Collecting and recording data

GEOGRAPHY
The seasons
Weather and climate

PHSE
Caring for living things
Showing respect
Taking responsibility

Glossary

abdomen The rear part of an ant's body that contains organs such as the stomach.

antennae The feelers on the head of an ant.

aphids Small bugs that suck sap from the leaves and buds of plants.

Arctic Circle An imaginary circle round the Earth, showing the southernmost edge of permanently frozen ground.

chambers The underground 'rooms' of an ants' nest.

grub (larva) The worm-like stage of an ant's life cycle.

marriage flight The one and only flight that young queen ants and male ants make in order to meet up and mate.

moult Shed the tough outer coat.

pupa The stage in an ant's life when it changes from a grub into an adult ant.

queen ant A large, female ant that mates with a male and lays all the eggs in an ant colony.

soldier ant A worker ant that is larger than the other workers, and whose job is to defend the ant colony.

worker ant A female ant that does not mate or lay eggs, but looks after the young ants, collects food and keeps the nest clean.

Index

The publishers would like to thank the following for their permission to reproduce photographs:
cover Tim Flach/Tony Stone Images, 4 Peter O'Toole/Oxford Scientific Films, 6 Oxford Scientific Films,
8 G Kramer/Oxford Scientific Films, 9 David Hosking/Frank Lane Picture Agency, 10 Dr Frieder Sauer/Bruce Coleman,
15 J A L Cooke/Oxford Scientific Films, 17 HPH Photography/Bruce Coleman, 19 Ken Preston-Mafham/Premaphotos
Wildlife, 20 Kim Taylor/Bruce Coleman, 21 Mantis Wildlife Films/Oxford Scientific Films, 22 Felix Labhardt/Bruce Coleman,
24, 25, 27 Ken Preston-Mafham/Premaphotos Wildlife, 28 Breck P Kent/Oxford Scientific Films,
29 Ken Preston-Mafham/Premaphotos Wildlife.